D0821778

King Cobras

Sam Hesper

PowerKiDS press.

New York

Published in 2015 by The Rosen Publishing Group, Inc.
29 East 21st Street, New York, NY 10010

First Edition

Editor: Caitie McAneney
Book Design: Michael J. Flynn

Photo Credits: Cover oariff © iStockphoto.com/oariff; p. 5 BENZINE/Shutterstock.com; pp. 6, 10, 21 Heiko Kiera/Shutterstock.com; p. 7 Chilli Productions/Shutterstock.com; p. 9 Dmitry Kalinovsky/Shutterstock.com; p. 11 Mark Newman/Lonely Planet Images/Getty Images; p. 13 Gregory Ochocki/Science Source/Getty Images; p. 15 pruit phatsrivong/Shutterstock.com; p. 17 Mattias Klum/National Geographic/Getty Images; p. 19 R. Andrew Odum/Oxford Scientific/Getty Images; p. 22 Matthew Cole/Shutterstock.com.

Library of Congress Cataloging-in-Publication Data

Hesper, Sam, author.
 King cobras / Sam Hesper.
    pages cm. — (Animal cannibals)
 Includes bibliographical references and index.
 ISBN 978-1-4777-5766-6 (pbk.)
 ISBN 978-1-4777-5768-0 (6 pack)
 ISBN 978-1-4777-5765-9 (library binding)
 1. King cobra—Juvenile literature. I. Title.
 QL666.O64H47 2015
 597.96'42—dc23
                         2014034261

Manufactured in the United States of America

CPSIA Compliance Information: Batch #CW15PK: For Further Information contact Rosen Publishing, New York, New York at 1-800-237-9932

Contents

Snake Eater

The king cobra is the world's longest **venomous** snake. This slithering beast is a natural predator and even eats its own kind, which is an act of cannibalism.

The king cobra is just one of the more than 3,000 kinds, or species, of snakes in the world. Snakes are reptiles, or animals with dry, scaly skin that lay eggs. Reptiles are cold-blooded. That means they take their heat from their surroundings. Around 600 species of snake are venomous. The king cobra truly is the king of these venomous snakes as it can grow up to 18 feet (5.5 m) long!

FOOD FOR THOUGHT

The king cobra may be the world's *longest* venomous snake, but it's not the most venomous snake. The inland taipan of Australia is often called the most venomous snake in the world.

The scientific name for the king cobra is *Ophiophagus hannah* (oh-fee-AHF-uh-guhs HAA-nuh). "Ophiophagus" is Greek for "snake eating." This name gives you the hint that the king cobra is a cannibal!

What Is a Cobra?

The name "cobra" is commonly given to many of the venomous snakes in southern Asia and Africa. Around 270 species are called cobras, but only around 28 of them are "true" cobras. King cobras aren't among the true cobras. True cobras are part of the reptile **genus** called *Naja*, while the king cobra is part of the genus *Ophiophagus*. In fact, it's the only member of this genus.

FOOD FOR THOUGHT

While other cobras have hoods, the king cobra's hood is longer and thinner than theirs. Also, the king cobra has 11 large scales on top of its head, while other cobras have only nine.

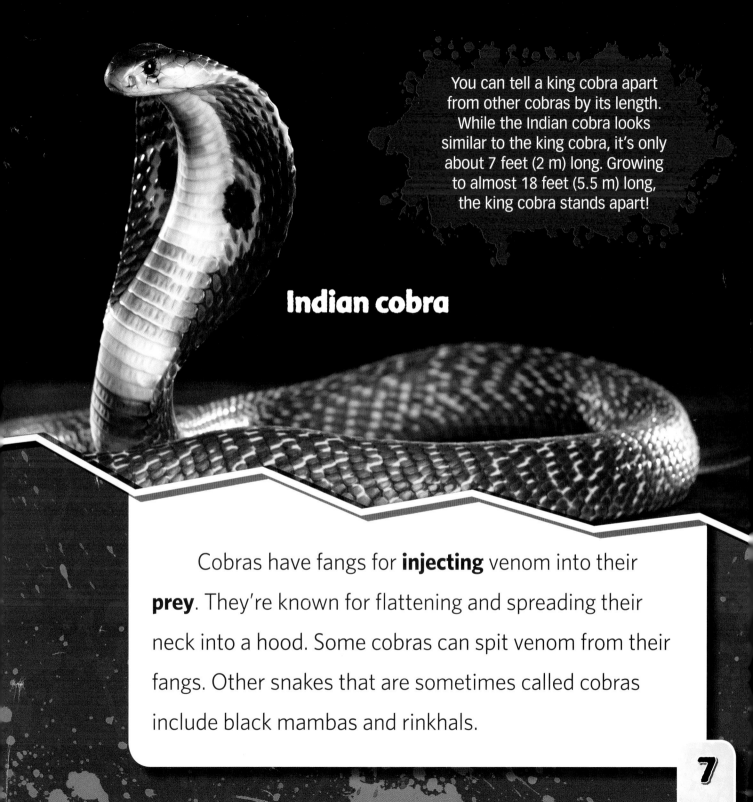

You can tell a king cobra apart from other cobras by its length. While the Indian cobra looks similar to the king cobra, it's only about 7 feet (2 m) long. Growing to almost 18 feet (5.5 m) long, the king cobra stands apart!

Indian cobra

Cobras have fangs for **injecting** venom into their **prey**. They're known for flattening and spreading their neck into a hood. Some cobras can spit venom from their fangs. Other snakes that are sometimes called cobras include black mambas and rinkhals.

Finding a King Cobra

If you're looking for a king cobra, you better like hot weather! Since king cobras are cold-blooded, they tend to live in warm **habitats**.

King cobras like the hot areas of southern Asia, such as India, Malaysia, Vietnam, southern China, the Philippines, and Indonesia. King cobras live in the rain forests of these countries. It's hot and wet in rain forests, but king cobras can also live in dry and grassy areas, too. They're able to move well in trees, in water, and on land. That's bad news if you're a smaller snake or animal nearby!

FOOD FOR THOUGHT

The cobra is an important **symbol** in Hinduism, which is a religion common in India and Southeast Asia. Cobras often stand for Shiva, or the god Hindus believe will destroy and re-create the world.

This snake charmer in India plays an instrument named a pungi to call to an Indian cobra. The "dancing" cobra isn't attracted to the sound of the pungi, but the movement of it. Snake charmers harm cobras when they remove a cobra's fangs or even sew their mouth shut.

Cobra Bodies

King cobras are strong snakes. They can lift part of their body off the ground when facing an enemy. King cobras also use their hood to scare enemies. The hood makes them look bigger and scarier. The hood is made of ribs in its neck. When a cobra is just slithering around or resting, the hood is gone.

FOOD FOR THOUGHT

Along with standing and spreading its hood, a king cobra will also hiss at its enemies. This hiss is so deep it can sound like a dog's growl.

Like all reptiles, king cobras are covered in scales. Their scales can be brown, green, black, and gray. King cobras often have markings shaped like the letter V. Their belly is often lighter in color and sometimes has bands.

When a king cobra stands up, it can be as tall as a person. Imagine meeting a venomous cobra eye-to-eye! It can strike its enemy or prey from far away when it's in this position.

Snake Senses

King cobras have incredible eyesight. When they lift their body off the ground, they can see about 330 feet (101 m) away. That means they can see prey from the length of a football field! They also use their senses of smell and taste to find their prey. Like other snakes, king cobras can "taste" the air with their forked tongue.

King cobras don't hear like we do. Instead, they sense **vibrations** through the ground. They're attracted to movement around them. That's why a cobra is more interested in the movement of a snake charmer's instrument than the sound.

FOOD FOR THOUGHT

If you're worried a king cobra can use its senses to hunt people, you're in luck. King cobras are actually very shy around people and would rather slither away than fight. They don't want you to come near them, so don't!

The king cobra's tongue has **receptors** on it that pick up on smells in the air. If it smells prey, it will flick its tongue to find the prey's direction. The king cobra's senses make it an unstoppable hunter!

Powerful Venom

King cobras use their venom to kill their prey. King cobras have small fangs, but they can inject enough venom at one time to kill a person in 15 minutes. In fact, there's enough venom in one king cobra bite to kill 20 people. King cobras can even inject enough venom to kill an elephant!

A king cobra's venom works by attacking its victim's brain and spinal cord. Once a king cobra bites its prey, the heart slows and the victim is unable to breathe. Fortunately for prey, a king cobra doesn't need to eat very often. A king cobra can survive months between meals.

Someone who's been bitten by a cobra must be injected with antivenin, which is made from cobra venom. In this picture, a person squeezes cobra venom into a beaker to make antivenin.

FOOD FOR THOUGHT

King cobra venom is used to make different medicines, such as aspirin and other pain relievers.

Hunting Other Snakes

A king cobra's favorite meal is another snake. They're just the right shape for a king cobra to swallow! Common prey include rat snakes and small pythons. These small snakes are easy prey for the mighty king cobra. If a king cobra doesn't find a snake to eat, it'll eat mammals, birds, and lizards. King cobras also eat other cobras and even other king cobras!

While hunting, a king cobra catches its prey and injects it with venom. When the prey is **paralyzed** or dead, the king cobra swallows its meal whole. It does this by **unhinging** its jaws to swallow big meals.

King cobras are **resistant** to many other snakes' venom, which is how they can eat other king cobras. In a match between king cobras, the larger cobra will likely be the winner, and the smaller will be dinner.

King Cobra Mating

King cobras usually mate, or come together to make babies, between January and April. During this time, female cobras lay a trail of scents called **pheromones** that tell males they're ready to mate. Since males are larger than females, the females want to make sure the males don't mistake them for prey. If it were any other time, the larger male probably wouldn't think twice about taking a bite!

Males may fight over females during mating season. They sometimes rise up and fight to push the other down. Once a male finds a female, they can mate. Afterward, the female lays between 20 and 40 eggs.

King cobra eggs, like most reptile eggs, have a strong shell that allows babies to grow inside the eggs on dry land.

Protecting Babies

Most snakes leave their eggs after laying them. It's easy for predators to snag a few for a meal. However, a female king cobra is different from other snakes. She builds a nest of leaves, lays her eggs, then piles more leaves on top. Then, she lays on the eggs to protect them from predators, such as mongooses. Male king cobras often stay in the area to protect the eggs, too.

After about two months, the mother leaves the nest before the eggs hatch. Scientists think she leaves because she's hungry and could give in to cannibalism. She doesn't want to eat her own babies!

FOOD FOR THOUGHT

Never go near a king cobra, especially while it's guarding its nest. While king cobras are usually shy, cobra parents will defend their young.

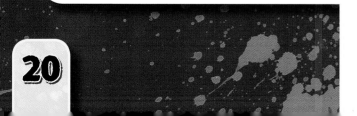

Baby king cobras are venomous and ready to hunt soon after they break out of their eggs.

Who Would Hunt the King?

Who would dare hunt a king cobra? The list is short. Cannibalistic king cobras and mongooses are usually the only animals that will attack an adult king cobra. Mongooses are quick moving and have thick skin and sharp teeth to protect themselves. They're also resistant to cobra venom.

However, the greatest risk to king cobras comes from people. People destroy king cobra habitats when they build new homes and businesses. People also kill king cobras for their skin. Some trap them for snake charming. While king cobra populations aren't yet in trouble, people should respect and save this mighty cannibal—the king of all snakes!

Glossary

genus: The scientific name for a group of plants or animals that share most features.

habitat: The natural home for plants, animals, and other living things.

inject: To force something into the body using a needle or sharp teeth.

paralyzed: Unable to feel or move.

pheromone: Matter given off by an animal that affects others of its species, especially when mating.

prey: An animal that is hunted by other animals for food.

receptor: A special cell in the body that takes in messages.

resistant: Not affected by something.

symbol: Something that stands for something else.

unhinge: To separate at a joint.

venomous: Having a poisonous bite.

vibration: A small repeated movement.

Index

A
Africa, 6
antivenin, 15
Asia, 6, 8

B
babies, 18, 19, 20, 21

E
eggs, 4, 18, 19, 20, 21
eyesight, 12

F
fangs, 7, 9, 14
females, 18, 20

H
habitats, 8, 22
hiss, 10
hood, 6, 7, 10

M
males, 18, 20
mongooses, 20, 22

N
nest, 20

O
Ophiophagus hannah, 5

P
people, 11, 12, 14, 22
pheromones, 18
predator, 4, 20
prey, 7, 11, 12, 13, 14, 16, 18

R
reptiles, 4, 6, 11, 19

S
scales, 4, 6, 11
sense of smell, 12, 13
sense of taste, 12
species, 4, 6

T
tongue, 12, 13

V
venom, 4, 6, 7, 11, 14, 15, 16, 17, 21, 22

Websites

Due to the changing nature of Internet links, PowerKids Press has developed an online list of websites related to the subject of this book. This site is updated regularly. Please use this link to access the list: www.powerkidslinks.com/ancan/cobr